Where Do Rivers Go, Momma?

CATHERINE L. WEYERHAEUSER

Mountain Press Publishing Company
Missoula, Montana
2016

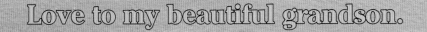

Love to my beautiful grandson.

Library of Congress Cataloging-in-Publication Data

Names: Morley, Catherine Weyerhaeuser, 1957- author.
Title: Where do rivers go, momma? / Catherine L. Weyerhaeuser.
Description: Missoula, Montana : Mountain Press Publishing Company, 2016.
Identifiers: LCCN 2016010562 | ISBN 9780878426560 (hardback : alk. paper)
Subjects: LCSH: Rivers–Juvenile literature.
Classification: LCC GB1203.8 .M65 2016 | DDC 551.48/3–dc23
LC record available at https://lccn.loc.gov/2016010562

PRINTED IN HONG KONG

MP Mountain Press
PUBLISHING COMPANY
P.O. Box 2399 • Missoula, MT 59806 • 406-728-1900
800-234-5308 • info@mtnpress.com
www.mountain-press.com

A little girl and her mother are out in a spring rain. They walk along a gurgling mountain stream. As the water hurries by, the little girl wonders.

Where do rivers go, Momma?

Rivers go where the water takes them. Gravity, the force that pulls everything downward, keeps water on a downhill path. Rivers can spill over a steep mountain slope, or they can move slowly, curving like a snake through flat landscapes. Rivers are like branches on a tree, getting bigger the closer they get to the trunk. Small creeks flow into bubbling brooks that empty into gentle streams that move into mighty rivers that dump into lakes and oceans.

Rivers are just one way water is stored and moved.

Water is everywhere.

It is in the air over the earth, in lakes and oceans, and in the ground under our feet.

The earth is called the blue planet because most of the earth's surface is covered with water.

Water can be a gas in the air,
moving with the wind.

In its liquid form, water drips as raindrops,
or soaks into the soil. A rainbow is the sun
away in the sky, causing the light to bend

runs in rivers, pools in ponds, shining on water droplets far into a colored arc.

When it is very cold, water freezes and can be lacy snowflakes, hard ice encasing a tree branch, or the slippery surface of a frozen lake.

In cold places,
such as on mountaintops,
thick piles of snow turn into
sheets of ice that can be as thick
as a ten-story building. The weight of the
ice causes it to spread and flow, forming rivers of
ice called glaciers. This slow-moving, frozen water
grinds up the rock below. Icy cold water flows
from the melting edge of the glacier and
spreads out in braided streams.

How old is water, Momma?

The water you see is as old as the earth.
Water that collects in a puddle today
once quenched the thirst of dinosaurs!

The sun heats the ocean. The water warms and becomes water vapor in the air. Plants and trees take water out of the ground through their roots and release it into the air as vapor. The vapor forms clouds that are moved by wind. If the air cools, droplets form in the clouds. And when the clouds get too heavy, rain, snow, or sleet falls on the ground. The rain either soaks into the earth and is stored in soil and rock layers, or it runs off into rivers and is stored in lakes and oceans.

Moving water can grind up rock along its path and carry it away. The wearing away of rock is

called erosion. Over millions of years, a river can carve a deep path through solid rock.

Where does the rock go, Momma?

Moving water carries rocks, sand, and mud. If the water slows down, sand and gravel drop to the bottom of the river. Where a river runs into an ocean or lake, the water fans out and slows down.

The falling sand and mud build up into a thick pile of new land called a delta. Ocean currents spread the sand into beaches along the shore.

What happens when water

Water moves slowly underground as it seeps into the spaces in dirt and rock. Some rocks soak up water like a sponge. Water in underground rocks is called groundwater, and the rock layers that

soaks into the earth, Momma?

contain a lot of groundwater are called aquifers. There is more water underground than there is in all the earth's lakes. People dig wells into aquifers to pump the water out to drink or for irrigating crops.

Can I drink this water, Momma?

Just like all animals and plants, you need water to live. But you should only drink filtered water. Even if a stream is cold and clear, tiny creatures you cannot see live in the water and can make you sick.

Why are some places so wet and other places so dry, Momma?

Mountains can cause rain to fall in one place and not another. Warm, moist air that blows off an ocean onto a mountain range will cool as it moves up the mountain's slope. As the air cools, the water vapor changes to water droplets, and it will rain and snow on the ocean side of the peak. Very little moisture is left by the time the air reaches the other side. The rainy side is thick with green plants. The dry side is usually brown, home to plants such as cacti, which can store water in their thick stems.

How we live affects the earth and its water cycle, sometimes in surprising ways and in unexpected places.

When it rains on a hillside cleared of trees and plants, rain carries large amounts of soil off into rivers. The muddy water can flow far away into an ocean and kill the fragile sea life.

Fertilizer on a field or garden can seep into lakes and
cause large amounts of algae to grow and fish to die.

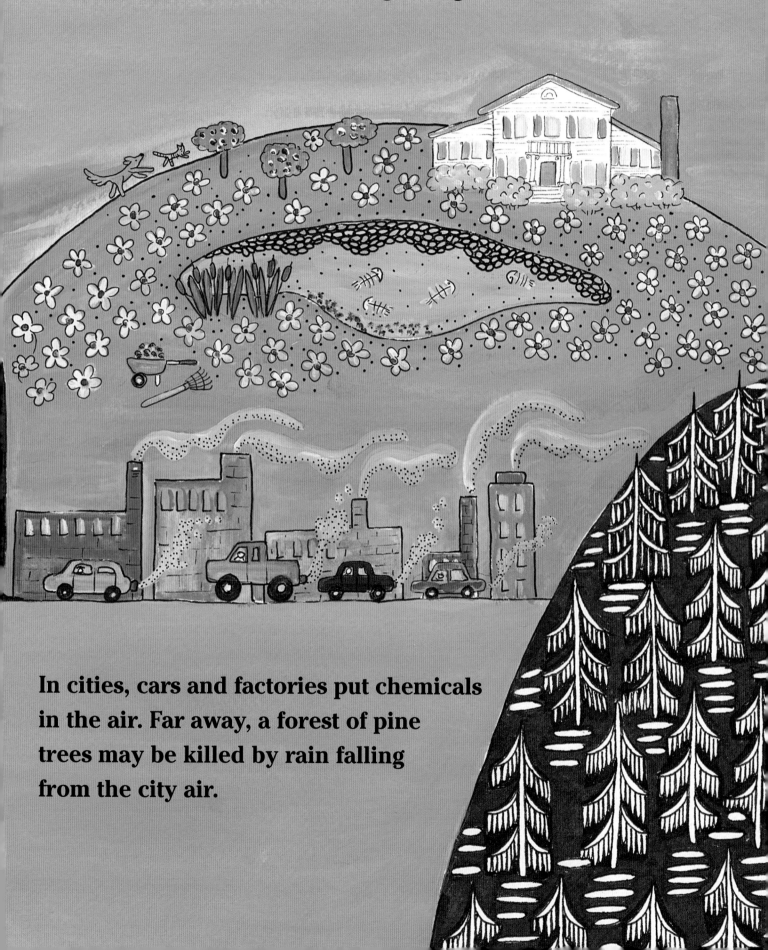

In cities, cars and factories put chemicals
in the air. Far away, a forest of pine
trees may be killed by rain falling
from the city air.

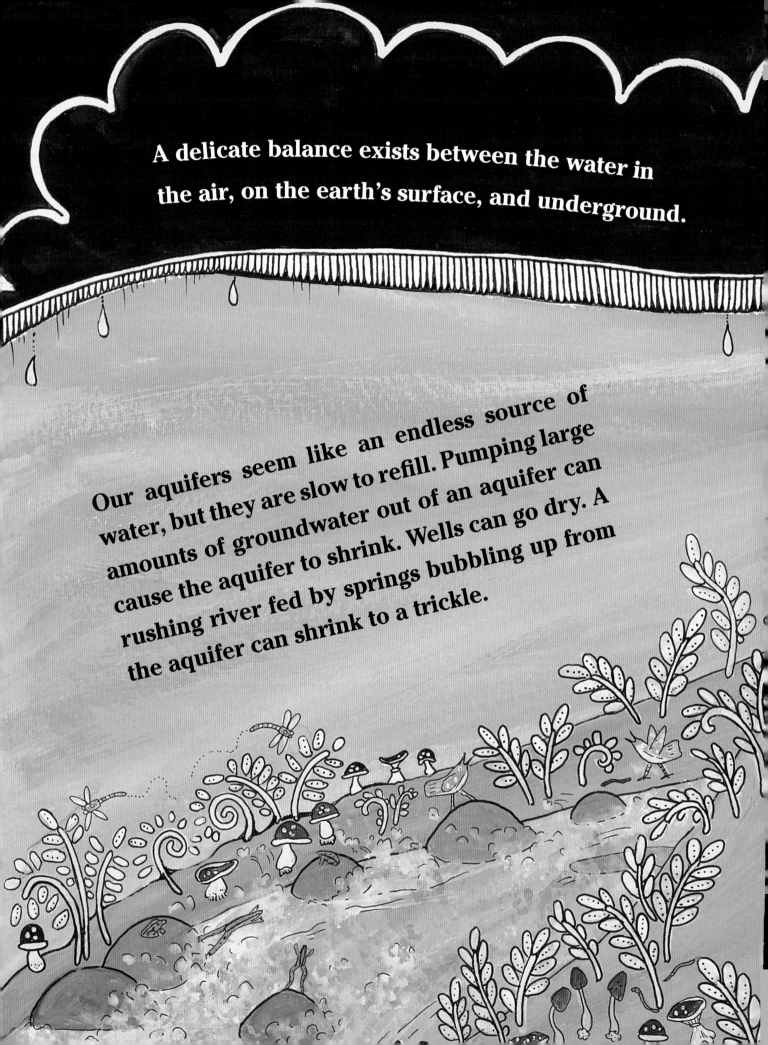

A delicate balance exists between the water in the air, on the earth's surface, and underground.

Our aquifers seem like an endless source of water, but they are slow to refill. Pumping large amounts of groundwater out of an aquifer can cause the aquifer to shrink. Wells can go dry. A rushing river fed by springs bubbling up from the aquifer can shrink to a trickle.

The little girl smiled at her mother and said, "Wow, Momma, it's amazing how many places rivers go. I want to be good to the earth so our water can be here forever!"

Real Rivers and Aquifers

MISSISSIPPI RIVER

The Mississippi River flows through the United States into the Gulf of Mexico. The river drains thirty-one states and part of Canada and carries large amounts of sand, silt, and clay. When the river reaches the gulf, the currents slow and the sediment drops out to form new land called a river delta. In recent years the river has carried large volumes of pollutants from agricultural runoff into the Gulf of Mexico, creating a dead zone where fish and other sea life cannot survive.

NILE RIVER

The Nile River, the longest river in the world, flows more than 4,000 miles from eastern Africa north through Egypt to the Mediterranean Sea. For thousands of years, heavy rain every autumn would erode nutrient-rich sediment and flood the river. When the rains stopped and the river level dropped, it would leave a layer of fresh sediment covering the floodplain and delta, making the land very fertile for farming. A dam was built on the Nile River in 1970 to control the flooding and generate electricity. The once-rich farmland, which had been replenished yearly, is now poor soil for crops and requires artificial fertilizers.

AMAZON RIVER

The Amazon River is the second longest river in the world, but it is the largest if you measure by the amount of water flowing through it. The Amazon drains much

of South America and is 50 miles wide where it flows into the Atlantic Ocean. It creates an enormous plume of silty freshwater that floats on top of the heavier, salty ocean water. Because of the strong ocean currents, the sediments in the river water are washed away and do not form a delta.

OGALLALA AQUIFER

The Ogallala Aquifer, one of the world's largest bodies of groundwater, lies beneath the Great Plains of North America, from South Dakota to Texas. It is used extensively for irrigating crops. Water is being pumped out of the ground six times faster than it is being recharged by rainfall and seepage. The aquifer may go dry in as little as twenty-five years. Farmers in the dry Texas Panhandle are already having to look into alternatives to irrigated agriculture.

NEW YORK CITY AQUIFERS

Long Island, home to much of New York City and surrounded by seawater, gets its freshwater from three main aquifers: the Upper Glacial, the Magothy, and the Lloyd. As the island's population has grown, water usage has increased, and the groundwater has been depleted. Seawater from the Atlantic Ocean has migrated into the aquifer, making the drinking water salty. Long Island communities have begun pumping cleaned wastewater back into the aquifer to try to keep out the salty seawater.

CATHERINE WEYERHAEUSER lives at the edge of a lake in Minnesota. As a child she hunted for agates around Lake Superior and took family trips to the Rocky Mountains, experiences that gave her a lifelong interest in the natural world. She has a BA in geology from Colgate University and a BS in elementary education from the University of Minnesota. While raising her children, she studied at the College of Visual Arts and the Minneapolis College of Art and Design in the Twin Cities. Catherine is the author of *Where Do Mountains Come From, Momma?*

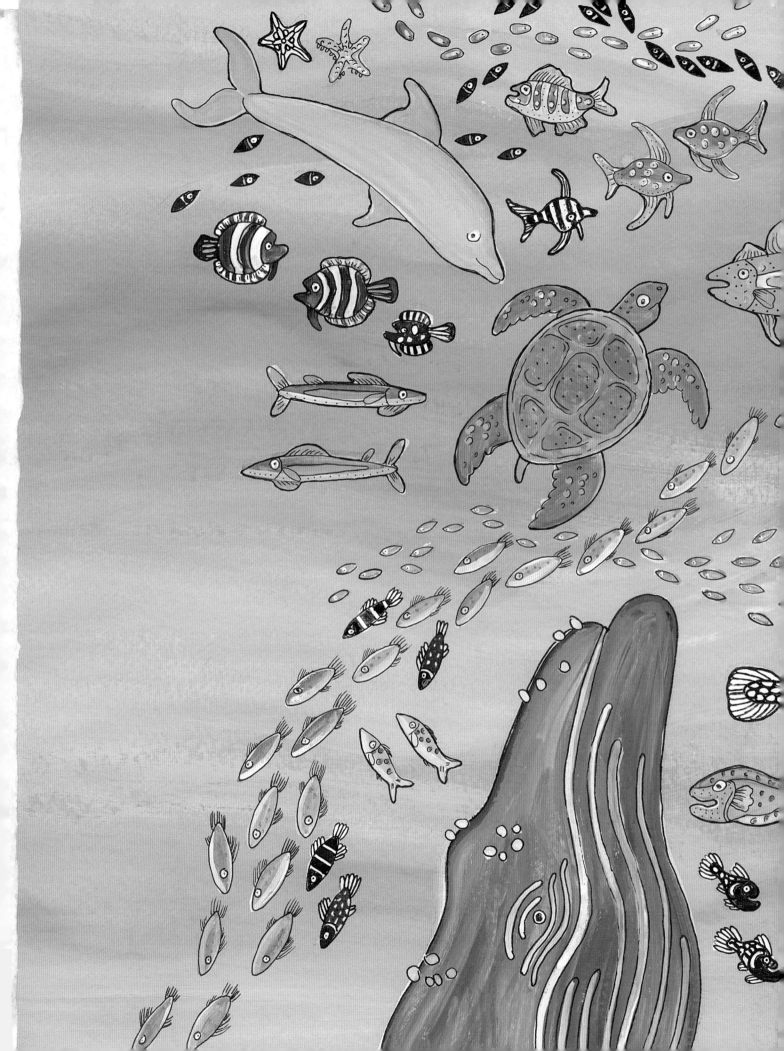